D1716573

A Primary Source Guide to

RUSSIA

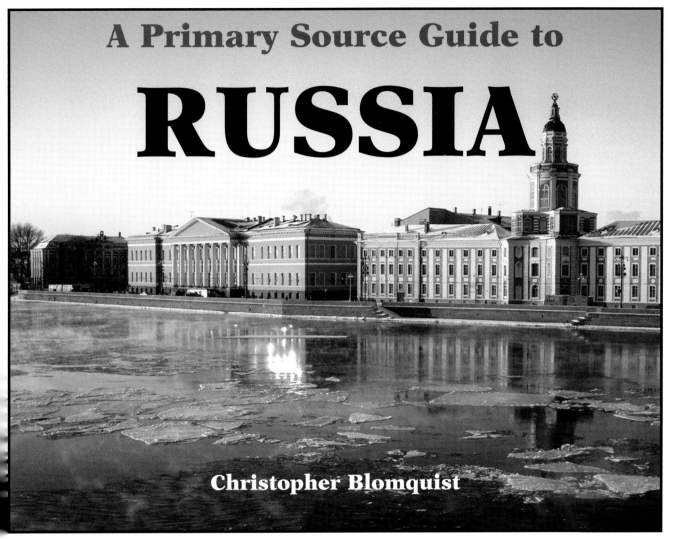

Christopher Blomquist

The Rosen Publishing Group's

PowerKids Press™
PRIMARY SOURCE

New York

For Rick, Manana, Nick and Michael Swanson

Published in 2005 by The Rosen Publishing Group, Inc.
29 East 21st Street, New York, NY 10010

First Edition

Editor: Kathy Kuhtz Campbell
Book Design: Haley Wilson
Layout Design: Michael J. Caroleo
Photo Researcher: Adriana Skura

Photo Credits: Cover Image © Frank S. Balthis Photography; p. 4 © 2002 Geoatlas, pp. 4 (inset), 10, 20 © Adam Tanner/The Image Works; p. 6 © Boyd Norton/The Image Works, (inset) © Staffan Widstrand/Corbis; p. 8 © Scala/Art Resource, NY, pp. 8 (inset), 9 © Hulton/Archive/Getty Images, p. 10 (inset) Peter Turnley/Corbis; p. 12 © Peter Blakely/Corbis Saba, (inset) © Hans J. Burkard/Bilderberg/AURORA; p. 14 © Getty Images News; p. 16 © Erich Lessing/Art Resource, NY; p. 17 © David Ball/Corbis; p. 18 © Robbie Jack/Corbis.

Library of Congress Cataloging-in-Publication Data

Blomquist, Christopher.
A primary source guide to Russia / Christopher Blomquist.— 1st ed.
    p. cm. — (Countries of the world, a primary source journey)
Summary: Text and photographs depict the history, government, culture, and traditions of Russia, the largest country in the world.
Includes bibliographical references and index.
ISBN 1-4042-2756-3 (lib. bdg.)
1. Russia—History—Juvenile literature. 2. Soviet Union—History—Juvenile literature. 3. Russia (Federation)—History—Juvenile literature. [1. Russia—History. 2. Soviet Union—History. 3. Russia (Federation)—History.] I. Title. II. Series.
DK41.B637 2005
947—dc22

                              2003021952

Manufactured in the United States of America

Contents

Arctic
Ocean

Siberia

Lena River

RUSSIAN FEDERATION

FINLAND

EUROPE

○ St. Petersburg

■ Moscow

URAL MOUNTAINS

BELARUS

↙ Kiev
UKRAINE
GEORGIA

Black Sea

Caspian Sea

TURKEY ↗↗
AZERBAIJAN

IRAN

ASIA

KAZAKHSTAN

Lake
Baikal

MONGOLIA

CHINA

Bering Sea

○ Vladivostock

NORTH
KOREA

*Pacific
Ocean*

ESTONIA

LATVIA

LITHUANIA

KALININGRAD
OBLAST

POLAND

BELARUS

4

A Giant Country

The Russian **Federation**, or Russia for short, is the largest country in the world. Its total land area is 6,592,800 square miles (17,075,274 sq km). Russia lies across two **continents**, Europe and Asia. Western Russia is part of Europe and eastern Russia is part of Asia. The Ural Mountains separate these two areas of Russia.

The Baltic Sea and eight European countries, including Belarus, Latvia, Estonia, and Finland, border western Russia. Russia is bordered by the Arctic Ocean in the north and the Pacific Ocean in the east. The Black Sea, the Caspian Sea, and the countries of Georgia, Azerbaijan, Kazakhstan, Mongolia, China, and North Korea border southern Russia.

Russia's land includes the small, unconnected area near Poland called Kaliningrad Oblast. *Inset:* St. Basil's Cathedral is the oldest building in Moscow's Red Square. It was built from 1555 to 1560.

Flat Lands and Freezing Winters

Russia is made up mostly of flat plains. A snowy, treeless tundra covers the northern part of the Russian territory called Siberia. The tundra, which is a cold plain with frozen soil, is Russia's least-populated area. The tundra can be as cold as -90°F (-68°C) in the winter. South of the tundra is the forest belt, or taiga. The northern taiga has pine forests and soil that is not good for farming. The taiga's southern half has maple and oak forests and better soil. Below the taiga is an area of grassy meadows called steppes. Most Russian farms are located on the steppes because they have rich, black soil. Southern Russia has mountain ranges and is warmer than the steppes and the taiga.

Russia has about 2 million lakes. Lake Baikal is the largest freshwater lake in Asia. It is the deepest lake in the world. Its deepest point measures 5,315 feet (1,620 m). *Inset:* Reindeer are raised on the tundra of northeastern Russia.

8

Mongols, Czars, and Communists

Around 1000 B.C., tribes from Europe and what is now Iran were living in Russia. By the A.D. 800s, Europeans called East Slavs and a **Viking** tribe called the Varangian Russes formed the Kievan Rus kingdom in Kiev. In 1237, Mongols, who were an Asian tribe, **invaded** the Rus kingdom and ruled for about 200 years. Ivan IV was crowned Russia's first czar, or grand prince and ruler, in 1547. Czars and **empresses** ruled for almost 400 years. In 1917, thousands of Russians stormed Czar Nicholas II's palace in Petrograd, or today's St. Petersburg. They killed the czar and his family in 1918 and set up a **Communist** government headed by Vladimir Lenin.

Empress Catherine II, called Catherine the Great, ruled Russia from 1762 to 1796. *Inset*: This 1917 announcement stated that Soviet workers and soldiers had taken over the government. *Above*: Czar Nicholas II, the last czar, is seen here in 1913 with his family.

9

The U.S.S.R.'s Rise and Fall

In 1922, Russia and three Communist **republics**, Byelorussia, Transcaucasia, and Ukraine, joined to form a new nation. Called the Union of Soviet Socialist Republics, or U.S.S.R., this nation became very powerful over the next 60 years. Dictators, or rulers who have total control over others, ruled the U.S.S.R. Dictator Joseph Stalin, who was in power from 1924 to 1953, forced people to give their land to the state. He had thousands of people whom he thought were enemies killed in acts called purges.

In 1985, Mikhail Gorbachev became head of the U.S.S.R. Though he gave people more freedom, some republic leaders wished to be independent. They formed the **Commonwealth** of Independent States in 1991.

In 1990, the Congress of People's Deputies, seen here in 1992, voted to allow non-Communist political parties in the U.S.S.R. *Inset:* Mikhail Gorbachev quit his post as president on December 25, 1991, and the U.S.S.R. ceased to exist.

Right: Fishers bring in a catch of sturgeon from Russia's Volga River. Sturgeon eggs are used to make a salty food called caviar.

ОГНЕОПАСНО!

ОГНЕОПАСНО!

The Russian Economy

For 70 years a Communist government owned all Russian businesses and controlled the prices of most goods. Since 1991, Russia has been building a modern and free economy. In 1998, the value of Russia's national money, which is the ruble, fell sharply. This drop made millions of people very poor. In recent years the ruble has gotten stronger and many Russian companies are growing. However, about one-quarter of Russia's 144,417,000 people are still very poor.

Key Russian **industries** include oil and gas drilling and the mining of coal, nickel, and iron. Russia is one of the world's largest producers of oil. Its wells produce 7.3 million **barrels** of oil each day. Russia's major food crops include wheat, potatoes, and sugar beets.

◄ Oil is purified in plants such as this one in Perm, Russia. *Above:* The 5-ruble note shows a monument in Novgorod that honors 1,000 years of Russian history.

The Russian Language

Russian is the official language of Russia and is the native, or first, language of more than 170 million people around the world. Russian is the language spoken by the most people in Europe. Russian uses a different system of letters from English. The Russian alphabet, which is also called the Cyrillic alphabet, is based on the Greek alphabet. In the eleventh century, the city of Novgorod was a center of writing. Most of Novgorod's people could read and write, and many authors lived in the city. While digging in Novgorod in 2000, scientists discovered three wax tablets that may be the oldest examples of writing in Russian ever found. The tablets, on which the **psalms** of David are written, date from the A.D. 1020s.

This wax tablet from the eleventh century holds some psalms of David that were written in Cyrillic. The use of soft wax, such as that on this tablet, made a writing method available to all social classes. Wax could be easily scratched with a tool.

16

Religion in Russia

About 108 million Russians are not members of any religion. Russia's remaining 36 million people are mostly **Christians** who belong to the Russian Orthodox Church. The early Russian Church was founded in 988. It used to

be run from the city of Constantinople, which was the center of the eastern Christian world. In 1448, Russian **bishops** broke away from Constantinople and stated their church's independence. Over the centuries the Russian Orthodox Church built many churches and **cathedrals**. The Communists were against religion and seized most church buildings and lands. Today the government has returned many of these properties.

Saint George and the Dragon is an icon, or religious picture. Painted in the late 1400s, it shows Saint George, who stood for the Russian princes, killing a dragon, which stood for evil. *Above:* This St. Petersburg church has onion-shaped roofs.

17

Russia's Beautiful Ballets

Russia has given the world thousands of artists and writers over the centuries. However, Russia may be best known for its great musicians and ballet dancers. One very famous and popular Russian composer, or writer of music, is Pyotr Ilich Tchaikovsky, who lived from 1840 to 1893. His ballets, such as *Swan Lake* and *Sleeping Beauty*, are still acted out all over the world. Another of Tchaikovsky's works, *The Nutcracker*, is presented every Christmastime by some of the world's best ballet companies. It tells the story of a little girl named Clara who dreams that her man-shaped nutcracker turns into a prince who dances with magical creatures. Russia's best ballet companies are Moscow's Bolshoi Ballet and St. Petersburg's Kirov Ballet.

◄ Members of Moscow's Bolshoi Ballet danced in *Romeo and Juliet*. The ballet *Romeo and Juliet* is about two young people who fall in love.

20

Russia Today

Russia has never been an easy place to live. From the Mongols to the czars to the Communists, the country's rulers have been unkind to Russians. Today a president, a **parliament**, and several courts run Russia. The parliament includes a lower house, called the State Duma, and an upper house, called the Federal Council. The Russian people elect the president and the 450 members of the State Duma for four-year terms. Russia's government is trying to improve the lives of its citizens. For example, in 2001, the State Duma passed a law that let Russians buy land for the first time since the Communists came to power. Russians are working hard to have a better tomorrow.

◀ This photo of Russia's capital city, Moscow, shows St. Basil's Cathedral and the redbrick walls of the Kremlin, or stronghold. Located in the middle of Moscow, the Kremlin contains three churches and several palaces.

Russia at a Glance

Population: 144,417,000

Capital City: Moscow

Largest City: Moscow, population 8,369,200

Official Name: Russian Federation

National Anthem: "Anthem of the Russian Federation"

Land Area: 6,592,800 square miles (17,075,274 sq km)

Government: Federal republic

Unit of Money: Ruble

Flag: The flag has a white stripe on top, a blue stripe in the middle, and a red stripe on the bottom. The red stands for bravery and love, the blue for honesty, and the white for goodness. Peter the Great first adopted this flag in 1705. From 1917 to 1991, the U.S.S.R. had a different flag until this one was used again.

Glossary

barrels (BAR-ulz) Containers with a flat top and bottom and curved sides.

bishops (BIH-sheps) Leaders of a faith, such as Roman Catholicism, who are ranked above a priest.

cathedrals (kuh-THEE-drulz) Large churches that are run by bishops.

Christians (KRIS-chunz) People who follow Jesus's teachings and the Bible.

commonwealth (KAH-mun-welth) A nation or state founded on what is right for the common good.

Communist (KOM-yuh-nist) Belonging to a system in which all the land, houses, and factories belong to the government and are shared by everyone.

continents (KON-tin-ents) The seven great masses of land on Earth.

empresses (EM-pres-ez) Female rulers of an empire, or several countries.

federation (feh-duh-RAY-shun) A group of governments that join to form a central government.

industries (IN-dus-treez) Moneymaking businesses in which many people work and make money producing a particular product.

invaded (in-VAYD-ed) Entered a place in order to attack and take over.

parliament (PAR-lih-mint) The lawmakers of a country.

psalms (SOMZ) Songs or poems of faith.

republics (ree-PUB-liks) Forms of government in which the authority belongs to the people.

Viking (VY-king) Referring to the Scandinavian sailors who attacked the coasts of Europe from the eighth to the tenth centuries.

Index

Primary Source List

Cover. St. Petersburg's Academy of Sciences and Kunstkamera, located along the Neva River. The Academy of Sciences was built by Giacomo Quarenghi between 1783 and 1789 for Catherine the Great. The Kunstkamera was founded by Peter the Great in 1714 to house his Cabinet of Curiosities. It was the first museum in Russia.

Page 4 (inset). Pokrovsky Sobor, popularly known as Church of the Intercession or St. Basil's Cathedral, Moscow. It was commissioned by Ivan IV (Ivan the Terrible) to celebrate his conquest of the Tatar city of Kazan in 1552.

Page 8. *Portrait of Catherine the Great Attired in Legislative Regalia in the Temple of Justice.* Oil on canvas, painted by Dmitry Gregorievitch Levitsky in 1783.

Page 8 (inset). "The Proclamation of the Revolutionary Committee of the Petrograd Soviet Workers and Soldiers Deputies announcing the overthrow of the provisional government and the transfer of power to the Petrograd Soviet." October 25, 1917.

Page 14. Wax-covered tablet on which the psalms of David are written in Cyrillic. Dates from 1000 to 1025.

Page 16. *Saint George and the Dragon.* Russian icon from Novgorod, late 1400s. Antwerp, Belgium.

Page 17. Church of the Resurrection of Jesus Christ, also called the Church on Spilled Blood or the Savior on the Blood Church. Built in St. Petersburg to honor the spot where Czar Alexander II was assassinated in 1881.

Web Sites

Due to the changing nature of Internet links, PowerKids Press has developed an online list of Web sites related to the subject of this book. This site is updated regularly. Please use this link to access the list:

www.powerkidslinks.com/cwpsj/psrus/

DATE DUE

SEP 2 5 2009			
OCT 1 5 2009			
NOV 0 9 2011			
DEC 0 1 2011			
JAN 2 0 2012			

FOLLETT